SITUATION LEARNING

STUDENT'S STUDY BOOK FOR SCHEDULE III B

MARIETTA LAING BIDDLE

ISBN 0-8388-1618-5 Printed in U.S.A.

April 2002 Printing

6 7 8 PAH 15 14 13 12 11

Code and read these words.

ow = (ō) one syllable

blow	low	sow
bow	mow	stow
crow	row	strow
flow	show	throw
glow	slow	tow
grow	snow	trow

---

ow = (ō) two syllables

aglow	elbow	marrow
arrow	fallow	mellow
barrow	fellow	minnow
bellow	follow	morrow
below	furrow	narrow
billow	gallows	pillow
borrow	hallow	sallow
burrow	harrow	shallow
callow	hollow	sorrow

sparrow	wallow	winnow
swallow	willow	yarrow
tallow	window	yellow

---

ow = ($\bar{o}$) compound words

crowbar	overthrow
fellowship	showman
landowner	snowflake
lowland	wheelbarrow
marshmallow	windowpane
overflow	

For reading only

bowl	thrown
flown	bestow
grown	disown
growth	shadow
own	widow
shown	rainbow
sown	tomorrow

1. If the north winds blow, will the sparrow and swallow fly low?

2. Mow the yard before the weeds grow rampant.

3. Show the little boy how to throw the darts and shoot with his bow and arrow.

4. The minnows darted about in the shallow pool, and the rabbit hid in his burrow.

5. As he rowed the craft beyond the narrow gap, she stood under the weeping willow tree and waved.

6. Tallow dripped from the yellow candle on the table, and he stared out of the window at the gallows.

7. That fellow must borrow a big truck to tow the car out of the snow.

8. Store the equipment below, and report to the first mate on deck.

9. She broke her elbow when she fell over the wagon.

10. He sat on a hollow log by a babbling brook and ate his lunch.

11. The warmth and glow of the fire made her forget her sorrow.

12. After he uses his harrow, the farmer will sow the seeds.

13. Some tides flow and ebb twice a day.

14. On the morrow shortly after the rooster crows, her sheets will billow from the line.

15. She slowly fluffed the pillow, as the mellow sound of the music filled the room.

16. That fallow land will not be planted this spring.

17. Will those fat pigs wallow in the mud?

18. The plow made deep furrows in the ground.

19. Follow the path into the woods.

20. The commander bellowed the orders to the confused troops.

21. If the window is stuck, use the crowbar to pry it open.

For reading only

1. Wash those dirty window panes!

2. Will the river overflow its banks?

3. Melt the marshmallows now and then fill the bowl with apples.

4. The birds had flown south before the snowflakes fell.

5. The landowner cleared the growth and underbrush from his property.

6. Has she thrown the ticket away?

7. Do you own a wheelbarrow?

8. How that tree has grown!

9. Is there a pot of gold at the end of the rainbow?

10. Will he disown his child?

11. Tomorrow the queen will bestow the award on the best rider.

Read these words.

Choose diphthong ow = (ou)
or
digraph ow = (ō).

ow = (ou)	ow = (ō)	ow = (ou) or (ō)?
brow	blow	arrow
cow	crow	elbow
how	glow	endow
now	slow	follow
prow	throw	grow
vow	pillow	minnow
allow	shallow	plow
fowl	bowl	scow
growl	flown	window
scowl	shown	yellow
bow	bow	brown
mow	mow	grown
row	row	owl
sow	sow	own

Spelling: Fill in the blanks with (êr) = er or or.

v____b

h____

p____k

w____k

cl____k

t____m

w____m

w____sted

p____fect

w____thy

w____d

w____th

w____ld

n____ve

h____d

w____st

f____n

w____ship

d____by

p____son

Code and read these words. oa = ($\bar{o}$) one syllable

bloat	float	loam	road
boar	foal	loan	roam
board	foam	loath	roan
boast	gloat	loathe	roar
boat	goad	moan	roast
broach	goal	moat	shoal
cloak	goat	oaf	shoat
coach	groan	oak	soak
coal	groat	oar	soap
coarse	hoard	oast	soar
coast	hoarse	oath	throat
coat	hoax	oats	toad
coax	load	poach	toast
croak	loaf	roach	

Code and read these words.

oa = (ō) two syllables

aboard

afloat

bemoan

cocoa

oakum

reload

reproach

---

oa = (ō) compund words

carload

charcoal

gunboat

lifeboat

oatmeal

overboard

railroad

roadbed

rowboat

seaboard

seacoast

switchboard

1. Will a boat float in a moat?

2. Coax, don't goad the mule.

3. He took an oath to tell the truth.

4. A toad hopped across the road.

5. Poach the fish and bake the roast.

6. Will a roan mare have a red foal?

7. Black loam is good for plants.

8. She likes to brag and boast about her team.

9. The truck with the big load travels coast to coast.

10. He will groan and moan if a bone sticks in his throat.

11. Frogs croak.

12. A roach skittered over the sink.

13. Sea gulls soar along the shore.

14. She will get a loan to pay her room and board.

15. Don't burn the toast or bake the loaf too long.

16. If he misses the goal, the coach will roar.

17. He rested in the shade of the big oak tree.

18. We watched the goat scamper to the top of the crag.

19. Soak the socks.

20. He will take his coat from the peg and roam the hills.

21. She hid the oar under the cloak.

22. He held the lump of coal in both hands.

23. Use foam to clean the rug.

24. The pink soap made a fine lather.

25. He fed the oats to his tan pony.

26. Joan was loath to broach the subject.

27. If the hunter shoots the boar, what will become of the shoat?

28. The oaf sailed the ship into shoal water.

29. He will save the groat instead of spending it.

30. The football fan became hoarse from too much cheering.

31. It was merely a hoax.

32. Don't hoard the coins.

33. Sal said, "I loathe coarse cloth."

34. When we were aboard ship we dressed for dinner.

35. The life jacket kept her afloat.

36. Don't bemoan the fact that he is late.

37. She ordered cocoa with her cake.

38. He used oakum to repair the seams of the ship.

39. Reload the rifle quickly.

40. Do not reproach the child if she makes a mistake.

41. He ordered a carload of carrots.

42. Use charcoal to grill the steaks.

43. The gunboats were used to set up the blockade.

44. He was startled from his sleep by the cry, "Man overboard!"

45. The railroad workers repaired the roadbed.

46. The waves lapped the shore as we drove along the seaboard.

47. He spent the weekend at the seacoast.

48. Call the switchboard to get the number.

49. The lifeboats were in the water long before the ship began to sink.

belt___ sash___

paper___ bunch___

book___ box___

drum___ dress___

tax___ tent___

gift___ glass___

inch___ imp___

fund___ fish___

match___ map___

Code and read these words. oe (ō)

doe	Joe	throes
floe	E. A. Poe	toe
foe	roe	woe
hoe	sloe	

Sentences to read oe = (ō)

1. When the car ran ovcr his dog, the boy was filled with woe.
2. The army marched out to meet the foe in battle.
3. As the shot rang out, the doe fled.
4. Joe yelled loudly when the hoe hit his toes.
5. The ice floe blocked the river.
6. E. A. Poc wrote exciting stories.
7. He ordered shad roe and sloe for lunch.
8. In the throes of defeat, the team members struggled to be good sports.

Vocabulary Review – optional
Put the number of the definition in the parentheses in front of the word it defines.

1. hollow noise or roar like that of a bull
2. pale reddish-yellow color
3. soft tissue
4. a tree with long, slender, hanging branches
5. to separate and drive off the chaff by means of wind
6. uncultivated
7. blessed; consecrated
8. not harsh; full and pure
9. not deep
10. trench made by a plow
11. fat of the ox or sheep extracted by melting
12. a hole in the ground made by certain animals for shelter

( )	1. mellow sound	( )	7. loud bellow
( )	2. fallow land	( )	8. tallow candle
( )	3. rabbit burrow	( )	9. sallow skin
( )	4. shallow stream	( )	10. weeping willow
( )	5. deep furrow	( )	11. hallowed ground
( )	6. to winnow grain	( )	12. bone marrow

Vocabulary Review — optional
From this list of words choose the correct word and fill in the blanks.

roam	foe	loam
shoal	foal	doe
throes	roe	boar
poached	coax	moat
shoat	woe	floe

1. Marooned on the ice ____________, the Eskimo looked longingly toward shore.

2. To ____________ in the woods made him happy.

3. She served ____________ eggs and shad ____________ .

4. Abundant crops grow in that black ____________ .

5. The ship's pilot must beware of the ____________ water.

6. Will that ____________ protect the castle from invaders?

7. A ____________ is a female deer.

8. He will go forth at dawn to meet his ______________ in battle.

9. Invite her to go with us, but don't ______________ her.

10. Did you hear his tale of ______________ ?

11. A ______________ is a male hog, and a little pig that has been weaned is called a ______________ .

12. Is the little ______________ a filly or a colt?

13. Involved in the ______________ of battle, he forgot everything.

Spelling: Fill in the blanks with (ŭ) = u or a.

g___m

___nder

___p

d___st

___mpire

n___t

m___st

s___n

___gly

___sher

___larm

p___rade

quot___

___way

c___reer

sod___

___round

col___

s___lute

___mbrell___

Code and read these words.

au = (au) one syllable

auk	fraud	maud
cause	gaunt	paunch
clause	haunch	pause
daub	haunt	sauce
daunt	jaunt	staunch
faun	laud	taunt
flaunt	launch	taut
		vaunt

---

au = (au) two syllables

audit	bauble	fauna
augment	because	gaudy
August	caucus	hauberk
aura	caustic	laurel
austere	Chaucer	Laura
Austin	faucet	launder
		maudlin

au = (au) two syllables (continued)

pauper	saucer	saunter
plaudit	saucy	

---

au = (au) three syllables

audible	authentic	laudanum
auricle	autopsy	nautical
aurora	fraudulent	tarpaulin

---

au = (au) four syllables

automatic	inaugurate

For reading only

One syllable		Two syllables
fault	maul	assault
Gaul	Paul	auburn
gauze	Saul	author
haul	vault	auto

1. A taut line held the boat in place.

2. On a jaunt to the woods, it is fun to pause and enjoy the fauna and flora.

3. The auk dives and fishes in the cold north.

4. We collected cups and saucers.

5. Can Lee make good hollandaise sauce?

6. Mark Twain wrote the story entitled *The Prince and the Pauper.*

7. Will she be able to augment her income in August?

8. We are planning an auto trip to Austin.

9. The author was concerned about the last clause in the agreement.

10. Will he perform the autopsy in the morning?

11. Which of Paul's shirts will we launder?

12. That Latin book tells us that all of Gaul is divided into three parts.

13. He donned his hauberk and rode into battle.

14. A certain aura surrounded her as the crown of laurel was placed on her auburn hair.

15. Mr. Gant is a gaunt man, and his wife is a staunch supporter of the good cause.

16. The girl in the gaudy green dress was fond of the shiny bauble.

17. A caucus was held on Friday.

18. Undaunted by the waves, he lifted the tarpaulin and launched the boat.

19. Because he was suspected of fraud, an audit was needed.

20. Do not taunt thc man with caustic remarks about his big paunch.

21. Will he study Chaucer's work next year?

22. The black and white dog sat on his haunches and begged for a bone.

23. Fix the leaky faucet.

24. After daubing paint on the walls and hearing a noise in the attic, the boys did not saunter but ran swiftly from the haunted house.

25. As she placed the stocks and bonds in the vault, her reply was barely audible.

26. Is that item authentic?

27. When will the plan for automatic retirement be inaugurated?

28. The accident was not his fault, but he will haul the car to the shop.

29. Will the tiger assault and maul his keeper?

Code and read these words. aw = (au) one syllable

caw	law	squaw
claw	maw	straw
craw	paw	taw
draw	raw	thaw
flaw	saw	yaw
jaw	slaw	

Advanced
For reading only

One syllable

awe	dawn	lawn	spawn
awl	drawl	pawl	sprawl
bawl	drawn	pawn	squawk
brawl	fawn	prawn	trawl
brawn	gawk	scrawl	yawl
crawl	hawk	shawl	yawn

Advanced
Two syllables

dawdle	Mohawk
hawser	Shawnee
lawyer	tawny

Compound words

crawfish	pawpaw
outlaw	seesaw

1. When the crow gave a loud harsh caw, the fox grabbed the cheese.

2. Martha will bring slaw and raw carrots to the picnic.

3. That cat has sharp claws.

4. Did Joan find the flaw in the fabric?

5. Draw a card and let's finish the game.

6. *Jaws* was the name of the film about a big shark.

7. A thorn in his paw caused the little white dog to limp about the yard.

8. Lee was unable to cut the wood with the rusty old saw.

9. Joe wants to study law.

10. The squaw decorated the blankets with quills, shells, and beads.

11. By noon, the sun will thaw the ice on the steps.

12. A taw, or shooter, is used to shoot marbles from the ring.

13. A wild gale caused the ship to heave and yaw like a straw in the wind.

14. Borrow an awl to punch a hole in the belt.

15. When Sally looked at the bones of the dinosaur, she was filled with awe.

16. We will study the Mohawk and Shawnee tribes.

17. The tawny puma waited silently to spring upon the deer and her fawn.

18. We will hike to the creek and hunt for crawfish.

19. Which fish swim upstream to spawn in fresh water?

20. In *A Tale of the Old West,* the outlaw robbed the bank before dawn and escaped to the foothills.

21. We sat on the lawn under the tree and ate the tasty pawpaws.

22. The sailor checked the hawsers on the ship and then went below to write in his log.

23. After the brawl, the man crawled to the bench and sprawled on it to rest.

24. Peggy and Susan ran to the park to play on the seesaw.

25. She stifled a yawn, took her shawl, and rode in a pony-drawn cart past the pawn shop.

26. We want to fish for prawns today, so don't gawk and dawdle.

27. The hawk will swoop down from the sky and catch the little gray mouse for his dinner.

28. The lady in the hoop skirt spoke with a soft drawl.

29. He scrawled his name at the bottom of the document.

30. The noise in the hen house was caused by the fluttering and squawking of the chickens.

Read these words.

a = (au) before l one syllable

all

ball

call

fall

gall

hall

mall

bald

false

halt

pall

small

squall

stall

tall

thrall

wall

malt

salt

scald

1. When smoke and fire filled the barn, all of the horses kicked the walls of the stalls.

2. After the sudden squall, she grabbed the mall and proceeded with the game.

3. As the music sounded in the hall, the undertaker placed the black velvet pall over the coffin.

4. The small pitcher frowned as the umpire called, "Ball three!"

5. Walt, the boy on stilts, seemed very tall.

6. Throw salt on the ice to prevent falls.

7. The bald man in the shiny boots ordered them to halt.

8. Scald the milk before adding it to the filling.

9. After the basketball game, the students met at the corner drugstore for a malted milk

Vocabulary Review – optional

Put the number of the definition in the parentheses in front of the word it defines.

1. a gust of wind, often with rain or snow
2. a marble to be used as a shooter
3. increase; make bigger
4. a young deer
5. severe; sharp
6. to steer wild when struck by a heavy sea
7. a trifling piece of finery
8. a person or craft that fishes
9. a part of the heart that receives blood from the veins
10. to waste time in idle lingering; to dally
11. unadorned; severely simple
12. stroll slowly or aimlessly

( ) 1. shiny bauble

( ) 2. sauntering along

( ) 3. austere life

( ) 4. heave and yaw

( ) 5. shrimp trawler

( ) 6. left auricle

( ) 7. sudden squall

( ) 8. little fawn

( ) 9. augment income

( ) 10. caustic remark

( ) 11. taw

( ) 12. don't dawdle

Code and read.
When is au used? When is aw used? When is a used?

auk
daub
daunt
faun
fraud
gaunt
staunch
taut
audit
augment
bauble
faucet
hauberk
launder
saunter

caw
claw
draw
flaw
jaw
law
paw
raw
saw
slaw
squaw
straw
taw
thaw
yaw

all
ball
call
fall
hall
small
squall
stall
tall
wall
bald
halt
malt
salt
scald

Check the check points.
Two checks = dropping e.
Add the suffixes.

The Dropping Rule

	Vowel Suffix?	Silent e?	Spelling
slope + ing			
dine + ed			
rope + ing			
fire + ed			
shape + ing			
fume + ed			
pave + ing			
blame + ed			
use + ing			
time + ed			

Check the check points.
Two checks = dropping e.
Add the suffixes.

The Dropping Rule

	Vowel Suffix?	Silent e?	Spelling
pine + ing			
file + ed			
slide + ing			
hope + ing			
slope + ing			
tape + ed			
glide + er			
plane + ed			
hide + ing			
ride + er			
drive + er			
noise + y			
dine + er			
grime + y			
serve + ed			

Check the check points.
Two checks = dropping e.
Add the suffixes.

The Dropping Rule

	Vowel Suffix?	Silent e?	Spelling
whine + er			
shade + y			
pure + ness			
joke + er			
carc + ful			
shine + y			
hope + ful			
shame + less			
safe + ly			
smoke + less			
mine + er			

Check the base word.
Do you drop the e or
double the consonant?

The Doubling Rule
The Dropping Rule

	Double	Drop	Spelling
sun + y			
big + er			
snap + y			
drag + ed			
quit + er			
shine + y			
tape + ed			
tap + ed			
can + ing			
cane + ing			
mop + ed			
mope + ed			

Pattern, divide, code and read.

VC'|CCV

1. district

1. emblem

1. lobster

1. escrow

1. instant

Pattern, divide, code and read. vc|ccv′

1. enclose

1. supplant

1. complete

1. perplex

1. distress

Pattern, divide, code and read.

VC'|CCV or VC|CCV'

1. c o n g r e s s 2. c o n g r e s s

1. s u b t r a c t 2. s u b t r a c t

1. s u l t r y 2. s u l t r y

1. t a n t r u m 2. t a n t r u m

1. e m p l o y 2. e m p l o y

Nonsense words to pattern, divide, code and read. VC'|CCV or V|CCV'

Blend initial in svllable

1. mafgron 2. mafgron

1. lonsnig 2. lonsnig

1. kipdrat 2. kipdrat

1. dafblop 2. dafblop

1. dasbrop 2. dasbrop

1. a r c t i c

1. b u m p k i n

1. e m p t y

1. g a u n t l e t

1. o i n t m e n t

Pattern, divide, code and read. vcc'/cv

1. o r d n a n c e

1. p a r t n e r

1. p l a n k t o n

1. s a n c t u m

1. s u m p t e r

Nonsense words to pattern, divide, code and read. vcc'/cv

Blend final in syllable

1. s o n t f o n

1. g a l p r o d

1. k e n d v o m

1. r u l d v i b

1. h i f t p e l

Divide, code, and read these compound words.

1. b a n d b o x

1. w i l d f i r e

1. d r i f t w o o d

1. p o r t h o l e

1. s w a m p l a n d

Divide, code, and read these compound words.

1. frostbite

1. cardboard

1. helpmate

1. crankcase

1. barnyard

Box the suffix, code, and read these words.

1. soundly

1. faultless

1. crisply

1. tactful

1. fastness

Box the suffix, code, and read these words.

1. b e l t l e s s

1. p l u m p n e s s

1. s c o r n f u l

1. t h a n k l e s s

1. s w i f t l y

Pattern, divide, code and read these words containing digraphs. VCC′|CV or VC′|CCV

1. athlete

1. anthem

1. merchant

1. kingdom

1. franchise

Pattern, divide, code, and read these words containing digraphs. VCC/CV or VC/CCV

1. b u c k r a m

1. e t h n i c

1. r i n g l e t

1. w o r s h i p

1. c a s h m e r e

Nonsense words containing digraphs to pattern, divide, code, and read. VCC′|CV

1. voshdeg

1. dackmoc

1. lethmut

1. rucklin

1. hingcad

Nonsense words containing digraphs to pattern, divide, code, and read. VC'|CCV

1. f e n t h e t

1. g o p c h a n

1. b a l s h u b

1. y u v t h i l l

1. k i m c h o f f

Code and read these words

g = (j) one syllable initial

gee gene gibe

gel gent gin

gem germ gist

---

g = (j) two syllables initial

gelid gentle germane′

gender gentry gibber

genet gerbil giblets

gentile German ginseng

---

g = (j) three syllables initial

gelatin genesis germańder

geminate genétic germinal

Gemini Genéva gibberish

general genocide Gibraĺtar

generate genuflect gigańtic

g = (j) one and two syllables

agent	logic	rigid
cogent	magic	tangent
congest′	margin	tragic
digest′	merger	turgid
digit	plunger	urgent
frigid	pongee′	vigil
largess	pungent	virgin
legend	regent	wager

---

g = (j) three syllables medial

agitate	indulǵent	origin
algebra	legislate	passenger
astrinǵent	longitude	refugee
cogitate	magen′ta	refulǵent
derringer	magistrate	tragedy
deterǵent	negligent	vegetate
indigent	nitrogen	vigilant

---

g = (j) four syllables medial

belligérent	intellígent
energetíc	origínal

1. Glance quickly over the report to get the gist, and study the details later.

2. The gentle boy cared for his gerbil.

3. In history class, we will study about the landed gentry.

4. He likened her gibes to the sting of arrows.

5. As he watched his troops march along the Unter den Linden, the German general wore his medals with pride.

6. He hopes the free balloons and paper hats will generate trade.

7. There will be a gigantic display of fireworks at the club on July 4th.

8. Genesis, the first book of the Bible, means beginning.

9. Don't gibber. Just chop the giblets before starting the sauce.

10. The worshiper will genuflect when he enters the church.

11. The statement, "As strong as the Rock of Gibraltar," refers to the British fortress in the south of Spain.

12. The secret agent left for Geneva at six o'clock.

13. It's urgent that the magistrate cogitate on the negligent attitude of the regent.

14. Which detergent did we choose?

15. I'll wager that the belligerent student will disregard the rigid rules.

16. It is a tragedy that the indigent refugee was forced to flee the land of his origin.

17. Kit's frigid reply broke the spell, and the magic of the moment was lost.

18. The lonely vigil at the sick child's bedside ended when morning came.

19. That tragic accident has long been a legend in these parts.

20. The passenger remained cool when the outlaw boarded the train, pointed the derringer at him, and shouted, "Hands up!"

21. Don't go off on a tangent. Remember the original plan. We must be vigilant.

22. The water is backing up in the sink. Quick! Use the plunger.

23. An intelligent energetic student, will help him with the difficult algebra problems.

24. Apply the astringent with a wad of cotton.

25. Write the notes in the margin.

26. The pungent odor of cloves filled the room.

27. Is there any logic in that last statement?

gem
gap
gin
got
gist

goblet
gibbet
gable
gully
gestic
gremlin

agitate
indigent
diligent

gun
germ
glad
gulch
grand

gender
goddess
ginger
genteel′
congeal′
suggest′

register
engineer′
passenger

g = (g)
In this list, g = (g) even though it comes before the letters e or i. Read these words which come to us from the Anglo Saxon language.

gear	gill
geese	gird
get	girder
giddy	girdle
gift	girt
gild	give
beget	linger
begin	longer
finger	stronger
hunger	target

Fill in the blanks with au, aw, or a.

st ________nch	sc ________ ld
________ dit	str ________
dr ________	h ________ berk
s ________ lt	h ________ ll
j ________	________ k
t ________ t	________ ll
w ________ ll	l ________
squ ________ ll	f ________ cet
l ________ nder	b ________ ble
t ________ ll	th ________

Code and read these words and phrases. <u>dge</u> = (j) one syllable final

badge	fudge	pledge
bridge	grudge	ridge
budge	hedge	sedge
cadge	judge	sledge
dodge	ledge	sludge
dredge	lodge	smudge
edge	midge	trudge
fledge	nudge	wedge

---

shiny badge	construct a bridge
don't budge	dredge for shrimp
dodge the ball	edge of the cliff
make fudge	stood on the ledge
hold a grudge	a hunting lodge
trim the hedge	nudge the sleeping man
wise judge	bound by his pledge
high ridge	to lift the sledge hammer
left a smudge	deposit of sludge
wedge of cake	able to trudge

1. His hat, boots, and shiny badge lay in a heap on the floor.

2. The engineer will construct the bascule bridge which will be used by both cars and ships.

3. Don't budge from this spot.

4. The men left before dawn to dredge for shrimp.

5. Nudge the sleeping man when he begins to snore.

6. When the cock crowed and the sun peeked over the high ridge, Carl started for the hunting lodge.

7. After he finished trimming the hedge, Kit accepted the offer of milk and a wedge of cake.

8. The wise judge instructed the members of the jury to consider all of the facts before a verdict was reached.

9. If he can dodge the ball, he will not fall into the tank.

10. The demented man stood on the ledge and stared at the crowd below.

11. Bound by his pledge, he kept the secret.

12. His dirty hand left a smudge on the window.

13. Life is too short to hold a grudge.

14. The tired boy was barely able to trudge up the hill.

15. Please make fudge for the candy sale.

16. In her effort to save the child, she clung to the sharp rocks and inched along the edge of the cliff.

Code and read these words.

ge = (j) one syllable final

age
barge
bilge
binge
bulge
cage
charge
cringe
dirge
flange
forge
fringe
gage

gorge
gouge
hinge
huge
large
lounge
lunge
merge
page
plunge
purge
rage
sage

Scrooge
serge
singe
splurge
stage
stooge
surge
tinge
twinge
urge
verge
wage

---

ge = (j) two syllables final

avenge
challenge
converge
diverge
divulge
emerge
engage

enlarge
enrage
estrange
exchange
expunge
impinge

indulge
infringe
oblige
rampage
revenge
submerge

1. Before the advent of trucks and planes, river barges took products to market.

2. If that log rolls out of the fireplace, it will singe the fringe on the rug.

3. Week after week, the old blacksmith stood before a flaming forge.

4. Scrooge said, "Bah! Humbug!"

5. Accept the sage's advice. Do not divulge the secret nor seek revenge.

6. "All the world's a stage" is a quote from a play by the Bard of Avon.

7. We felt a twinge of sadness and were on the verge of tears as we waved farewell to Flora and Fran.

8. Lunge, parry, and remise are all fencing terms.

9. Hamlet, the Prince of Denmark, was called upon to avenge his father's murder.

10. I urge each of you to help the exchange student get acquainted with her classmates.

11. What is the minimum wage now?

12. How much will he charge to fix the hinge?

13. He did not cringe as the mob surged forward.

14. If all the members converge on the city in June, it will be a challenge to find rooms for them.

15. Sadness filled the air when the dirge was played.

16. That number will be listed in the yellow pages.

17. Amber Locks was the child, and Shuffle Shoon represented old age.

18. Pump the water from the bilge and patch the hole.

19. Let's go on a shopping binge next Thursday.

20. "See this bulge? I must eat less," said Ada.

21. She sang about a nightingale in a gilded cage.

22. Don't gorge. Gout may be the result.

23. Engage the large lounge, and we will meet to discuss the merger.

24. Carl missed his footing and plunged from the cliff into the icy water.

25. If you indulge the spoiled child, you may be obliged to correct her later.

26. The paths diverge beyond that tree.

27. After her rampage, Jill's rage subsided.

28. The sailor told a story about a mermaid who emerged from the sea to sit on a rock and watch the ships.

29. Check the lines before the diver submerges for the last time.

Vocabulary Review — optional

Put the number of the definition in the parentheses in front of the word it defines.

1. convincing
2. a command used to guide teams to turn right
3. to blot out or rub out
4. strong; sharp; biting
5. to carry; to peddle; to beg
6. appropriate
7. a rim
8. mud
9. liberal gift
10. inflated; bloated
11. shining; glowing; resplendent
12. twilled worsted fabric

( ) 1. gee

( ) 2. germane

( ) 3. turgid

( ) 4. cadge

( ) 5. largess

( ) 6. expunge

( ) 7. flange

( ) 8. pungent

( ) 9. scrgc

( ) 10. cogent

( ) 11. sludge

( ) 12. refulgent

____outh	lu____id	su____pend
____afe	re____ede	e____cort
____uffix	bi____eps	ca____cade
____ift	de____ide	bri____ket
____eek	re____ent	pro____pect
____olvent	gro____er	clu____ter
____ingle	re____ite	ba____ket
____ampan	pre____ept	ab____orb
____ulk	ran____id	in____ult
____ettle	pla____id	ma____cot
____ell	pre____inct	pa____tern
____ilent	de____ent	pla____ter
____ummer	pre____ede	jet____am
____and	sin____ere	cat____up
____leep	ex____ept	bli____ter

blĕ___
kĭ___
glă___
exprĕ___
addrĕ___
profĕ___
tŏ___
confĕ___
recĕ___
succĕ___
excĕ___
accĕ_
goddĕ___
mĭ___
drĕ___

trā___
spī___
prodū___
rā___
devī___
effā___
prī___
spā___
ī___
dī___
redū___
plā___
rī___
fā___
entī___

goo___
hou___
sen___
ver___
caboo___
defen___
rever___
blou___
expen___
impul___
loo___
ten___
dou___
noo___
mou___

re ________ ede	pre ________inct
________ outh	e ________ cort
ca ________ cade	lu ________ id
pro ________ eed	________ afe
bri ________ ket	bi ________ eps
________ ettle	________ uffix
gro ________ er	de ________ ide
________ ulk	ca ________ ket
clu ________ ter	________ ift
pro ________ pect	________ eek
________ ampan	su ________ pend
re ________ ite	re ________ ent
________ ingle	________ olvent
pre ________ ept	

hou ________	effā ________
devī ________	sen ________
blĕ ________	kĭ ________
rā ________	ver ________
addrĕ ________	recĕ ________
goo ________	spī ________
trā ________	glă ________
produ̅ ________	profĕ ________
defen ________	rever ________
caboo ________	blou ________

pa _______ tern	pla _______ id
mĭ _______	rī _______
de _______ ent	expen _______
_______ en _______	_______ ilver
pla _______ ter	plā _______
noo _______	drĕ _______
_______ ell	ten _______
_______ ilent	_______ and
dou _______	loo _______
fā _______	exprĕ _______
pre _______ ede	rever _______
entī _______	redū _______
recĕ _______	_______ leep
_______ olve	ga _______ ket
_______ ummer	li _______ en _______

Code and read these words.

knack	knickers	knop
knacker	knife	knosp
knap	knight	knot
knave	knish	knout
knead	knit	know
knee	knob	knuckle
kneel	knock	knur
knell	knoll	knurl
knapweed	knick-knack	knockout
kneecap	knighthood	knothole
gnarl	gnash	gnaw
gnarled	gnat	gnome
		gnu
align	cologne	malign
assign	condign	resign
benign	consign	sign
campaign	design	

1. When Joan fell off her bike, she skinned her knees and her knuckles.

2. What is a knout?

3. She will knead the clay before she throws it on a potter's wheel.

4. Dana likes to knit socks.

5. Shine the knob and sharpen the knife.

6. Sir Galahad was a brave Knight of the Round Table.

7. Overhand, slip, square, and sheepshank are the names of some of the many kinds of knots.

8. Jeff has a knack for putting.

9. When the knacker appeared at the top of the knoll, Jed quickly hid his horse.

10. Which knave stole the tarts and ran away?

11. Did the knockout take place in the fifth round?

12. The man will kneel and the queen will say, "I dub thee knight."

13. The small boy stood on a box to reach the knothole and watch the game.

14. When there was a loud knock, she quickly returned the knick-knack to the shelf.

15. A little boy in knickers peered back at us from the pages of the old album.

16. I know he broke his kneecap in the accident.

17. In *Elegy,* Gray speaks of a knell tolled for a parting day.

18. The gnarled old oak tree stood by the gate like a silent sentry.

19. After he lost the bet, the irate man gnashed his teeth and paced around the room.

20. Swat the gnats before the picnic is spoiled.

21. If the rats gnaw the rope, it may set the boat afloat.

22. Deep in the cavern, the little old gnome kept the gems locked in chests.

23. Last Friday I went to the zoo and saw a gnu.

24. Can he align the wheels by five o'clock?

25. If he resigns now, will he be able to take part in the campaign?

26. Good news! The tumor was benign.

27. The dress design was worthy of the large fee, and he was happy to sign the check.

28. When will he assign the seats?

29. Don't malign me before the comittee.

30. Which cologne does she prefer?

Vocabulary Review — optional

Homonyms are words that sound alike but are spelled differently and have different meanings. From this list of homonyms choose the correct one, and answer the questions below.

knap — nap	knell — Nell
knave — nave	knight — night
knead — need	know — no

gnome — Nome

1. Which means to be certain? ____________________

2. Which means opposite of yes? ____________________

3. Which means a lack of something? ____________________

4. Which means to work and press into a well-mixed mass? ____________________

5 Which means a short sleep? ____________________

6. Which means a top or crest (of a hill)? ____________________

7. Which is a city in Alaska? ____________________

8. Which mean a little old man, a troll? ____________________

9. Which means the jack in a deck of cards?______________

10. Which means part of a church?______________

11. Which is a girl's name?______________

12. Which means a sound announcing the end of something?______
____

13. Which means the time from dusk to dawn?______________

14. Which means the man who in olden times was rewarded with high rank for serving his king?______________

Read the sound picture and spell the word correctly.

(kōd) ______________________________

(snĭf) ______________________________

(koin) ______________________________

(thou′ zănd) ______________________________

(măn′ ẽr) ______________________________

(hwīn) ______________________________

(kwā′ vẽr) ______________________________

(sō′ dȧ) ______________________________

(foi′ b'l) ______________________________

(chĭngk) ______________________________

(dĭ vīd′) ______________________________

(boun′ tĭ) ______________________________

(prō fĕs′) ______________________________

(kŏn′ voi) ______________________________

(hū mān′) ______________________________

Read the sound picture and spell the word correctly.

(chōz) ____________________

(măch) ____________________

(vălv′) ____________________

(plou) ____________________

(ē vŏlv′) ____________________

(ȧ jär′) ____________________

(jô) ____________________

(rīs) ____________________

(gär′ b'l) ____________________

(slō) ____________________

(jĭn′ jẽr) ____________________

(ăb sôrb′) ____________________

(plĕj) ____________________

(bŏks) ____________________

(jŭj) ____________________

Read the sound picture and spell the word correctly.

(rē sīt′) ____________________

(blĕs) ____________________

(jī găn′ tĭk) ____________________

(lŏk) ____________________

(gär′ lĭk) ____________________

(yĕl′ ō) ____________________

(pāj) ____________________

(ô dĭt) ____________________

(bŭlj) ____________________

(kāk) ____________________

(kôl) ____________________

Code and read these words.
Bracket final stable syllable.

Unaccented -age as final syllable in a baseword.

adage
advantage
average
beverage
cabbage
carnage
cartilage
damage
forage
garbage
hostage
image
luggage

manage
message
pillage
ravage
rummage
salvage
sausage
savage
umbrage
vantage
village
vintage
visage

Box the suffix and read these words.

Suffix -age

amperage
assemblage
baggage
bandage
brokerage
coinage
dosage
drainage
passage
pasturage

patronage
peerage
personage
pilgrimage
plumage
postage
pottage
storage
usage
vicarage

1. The old adage, "Look before you leap," offers good advice.

2. Ken takes advantage of every opportunity to travel.

3. What is the average age of the participants?

4. Which beverage does he prefer?

5. Jiggs was fond of corned beef and cabbage.

6. After the carnage of battle, the troops pillaged and ravaged the village.

7. The cartilage in his knee was damaged in the football game.

8. While foraging for food in the forest, the hermit and savage met.

9. After the terms were met, the hostage was released.

10. The image in the mirror smiled back at her.

11. Send the message now.

12. See what can be salvaged from the fire and take it to the rummage sale.

13. He enjoyed the vintage wine, cheese, and small sausages.

14. Nell took umbrage at Ned's rudeness.

15. *Vantage Point* is the title of a book written by President Johnson.

16. The memory of her visage remained with him long after she had left.

17. The number of august personages attending the assemblage almost overwhelmed the speaker.

18. What is the charge for the extra postage?

19. He will place his order with the brokerage firm in the morning.

20. Can you read *Northwest Passage*?

21. As soon as the guests arrive, he will carry the baggage into the vicarage.

22. The nurse will administer the correct dosage and then change the bandage.

23. His supper consisted of hard crusted rolls and a bowl of pottage.

24. He hoped to be cured when he made his pilgrimage to the shrine in France.

25. The peacock vainly displayed his plumage.

26. Bring the boxes from the storage room, and we will unpack them.

27. What is the value of the coinage?

28. The note at the bottom of the program said, "Thank you for your patronage."

29. Is he a member of the British peerage?

30. Will Greg be able to rent more pasturage for his cattle?

31. That bad presage seemed to spell doom for the project.

32. The book showed marks of hard usage.

Code and read these words.

ea = (ĕ) one syllable

bread	death	spread
breadth	dread	stead
breast	head	stealth
breath	health	sweat
dead	lead	thread
deaf	meant	threat
dealt	read	tread
	realm	wealth

---

ea = (ĕ) two syllables

abreast	leather	steady
ahead	leaven	sweater
behead	meadow	treadle
feather	measure	treasure
heather	peasant	weapon
heaven	pleasant	weather
heavy	pleasure	zealot
instead	ready	

Three syllables	Compound
already	bedstead
endeavor	breakfast
	commonwealth

1. Bread is called the staff of life.

2. It was a pleasure to have a warm red sweater when the heavens were cloudy and the weather turned cold.

3. Did Yankee Doodle have a feather in his cap?

4. Why did King Henry VIII wish to behead his wife?

5. I meant to inquire about her health.

6. Which car is ahead as they round the bend?

7. It's a threat to his safety if the tread on the tires is worn smooth.

8. The queen of the realm celebrated her silver jubilee.

9. As they were hitched to the troika, the horses stood three abreast.

10. Which weapon did he choose?

11. She needs a steady hand to thread the needle.

12. He held his breath and mopped the sweat from his brow as the dealer dealt the last card.

13. As she read the funny story, a smile spread across her face.

14. The stealth with which he approached the platform showed that he was filled with dread.

15. When he remarked that her cake was as heavy as lead, Stella wanted to hit Jed on the head.

16. The pleasant memory filled her mind, but her foot never left the treadle.

17. Three fish swam in a stream in the meadow.

18. Is she ready? We are already late for breakfast.

19. The peasants toiled hard from dawn until dark.

20. Her plea fell on deaf ears.

21. Longfellow compares death to a reaper.

22. Congreve wrote, "Music has charms to soothe a savage breast."

23. What is the depth and breadth of her feeling for him?

24. Cathy and Heathcliff met on the heather-filled moors.

25. Long John Silver, the pirate, hoped to find Captain Flint's treasures.

26. Let's insist on leather instead of plastic for the binding.

27. His endeavor to complete the assignment stood him in good stead with the leaders of the commonwealth.

Vocabulary Review — optional
From the words at the top of this page select the ones that are associated with the words at the bottom of the page and copy in the blank.

sweater	leather	realm	feather
ahead	pleasant	pleasure	stead
treadle	measure	leavening	breakfast

1. tape ____________________

2. ____________________ jacket

3. queen's ____________________

4. light as a ____________________

5. ____________________ agent

6. forge ____________________

7. cashmere ____________________

8. ____________________ surprise

9. stand in good ____________________

10. continental ____________________

11. foot ____________________

12. ____________________ trip

Choose ea = (ē) or ea = (ĕ)
List these words in the correct column. Use your copying procedures.

health
bread
steady
beaver
year
meat
leather
deal
stream
tread
meadow
spread
heat
dread
team
sea
veal
heaven
wealth
please

ea = (ē)	ea = (ĕ)
1.	1.
2.	2.
3.	3.
4.	4.
5.	5.
6.	6.
7.	7.
8.	8.
9.	9.
10.	10.

Read these words.

throw

now

grow

shallow

endow

yellow

pillow

vow

mellow

follow

sow

bow

row

mow

Choose ow = (ou) or ($\bar{o}$).

window

blow

allow

show

fellow

snow

plow

borrow

how

minnow

sow

bow

row

mow

Code and Read.

acquit´ + ed	acquitted
befit´ + ing	befitting
confer´ + ing	conferring
distil´ + er	distiller
excel´ + ed	excelled
forgot´ + en	forgotten
impel´ + ed	impelled
infer´ + ed	inferred
reset´ + ing	resetting
submit´ + ed	submitted
transmit´ + er	transmitter
upset´ + ing	upsetting

Code and Read.

allot´ + ed	allotted
al´ter + ed	altered
bal´lot + ing	balloting
control´ + er	controller
deter´ + ed	deterred
en´ter + ed	entered
expel´ + ed	expelled
gar´den + er	gardener
inter´ + ed	interred
pep´per + y	peppery
refer´ + ing	referring
wan´der + er	wanderer

Check the check points.
Three checks = final consonant doubled.

Doubling Rule.
Two Syllable Words.

	Vowel Suffix	b.w. 1 cons. 1v̆	Accent 2 syl.	Code and Read Words
begin + er				beginner
open + ed				opened
number + ed				numbered
forget + ing				forgetting
allot + ment				allotment
transmit + ing				transmitting
regret + ed				regretted
admit + ing				admitting
market + ing				marketing
forbid + en				forbidden
omit + ed				omitted
commit + ment				commitment

Check the check points.
Three checks = final consonant doubled.

Doubling Rule.
Two Syllable Words.

	Vowel Suffix	b.w. 1 cons. 1v̆	Accent 2 syl.	Code and Read Words
permit + ed				permitted
appoint + ment				appointment
resist + er				resister
trumpet + er				trumpeter
relent + less				relentless
carpet + ing				carpeting
offer + ed				offered
master + ful				masterful
rebel + ing				rebelling
avoid + ed				avoided
accent + ing				accenting
maroon + ed				marooned
accept + ed				accepted

Check the check points.
Three checks = final consonant doubled.

Doubling Rule.
Two Syllable Words.

	Vowel Suffix	b.w. 1 cons. 1$\breve{v}$	Accent 2 syl.	Code and Read Words
defer + ment				deferment
adroit + ly				adroitly
plaster + er				plasterer
support + ed				supported
happen + ing				happening
lampoon + er				lampooner
select + ing				selecting
excel + ed				excelled
applaud + ing				applauding
silver + y				silvery
propel + er				propeller
event + ful				eventful
report + er				reporter

Code and read these words.

ie = ($\bar{e}$) one syllable

bier
brief
chief
fief
field
fiend
fierce
frieze

grief
grieve
lief
liege
mien
niece
piece
pier

pierce
priest
shield
shriek
siege
thief
tier
wield
yield

---

ie = ($\bar{e}$) two syllables

achieve
belief
believe

besiege
cashier
Diesel
frontier

relief
relieve
reprieve
retrieve

---

ie = ($\bar{e}$) three syllables

cavalier

financier

1. The charming lady wore a green dress, and golden loops adorned her pierced ears.

2. His windshield wipers dragged and scraped as the rain pelted against the window.

3. Do you remember when we fished from the end of the old wooden pier?

4. Uncle Thad, a man of kindly mien, read a story to us after dinner.

5. The fortress fell after a brief siege.

6. The priest's beliefs differed from hers.

7. A blanket of grief enveloped her when she saw the bier.

8. Burning a mixture of air and crude oil, the huge diesel truck lumbered along the highway.

9. It was a false alarm, so the relieved cashier unlocked the drawer and relaxed.

10. What foul fiend committed such a dastardly act?

11. Will she yield to her desire for a second piece of cake?

12. Time is a thief who steals from all of us.

13. The weathered old chief remembered the days when buffalo roamed the frontier.

14. His niece holds a lien on the property.

15. The fief was granted to the knight by his liege lord.

16. The sight of the fierce beast evoked a shriek from the scared girl.

17. Place the replica of the bride and groom on the top tier of the wedding cake.

18. That fencer wields his foil with skill.

Vocabulary Review – optional

Homonyms are words that sound alike but are spelled differently and have different meanings. From this list of homonyms choose the correct one, and answer the questions below.

bier – beer	piece – peace
lief – leaf	pier – peer
mien – mean	tiers – tears

1. Which means a support for a bridge span, or a structure over the water used as a landing place? ____________________

2. Which means one of the same rank, an equal? ____________________

3. Which is part of a plant or tree? ____________________

4. Which means gladly, willingly? ____________________

5. Which means the drops of salt water that fall when you cry?

____

6. Which means rows or layers? ____________________

7. Which is the frame on which a coffin is placed? ______________

8. Which is a drink? ______________

9. Which means to intend or have in mind? ______________

10. Which means air, manner, looks? ______________

11. Which means a fragment or part? ______________

12. Which means opposite of war? ______________

Spelling - Fill in the blanks with j or g

______ ibe	______ ist
______ ene	______ erm
______ oggle	______ asper
______ in	______ entle
______ ump	______ iblets

Fill in the blanks with dge or ge

wā ______	dŏ ______
brĭ ______	ā ______
ver ______	ĕ ______
loun ______	stōō ______
hĕ ______	rĭ ______
bă ______	lŏ ______
gou ______	sin ______
lar ______	for ______
hū ______	bul ______
fŭ ______	bŭ ______

Spelling - Review generalizations (k), (ch), (j)
Fill in the blanks and notice that the longer spellings for these sounds occur in the final position in monosyllables immediately after one short vowel.

(k)

//ck, k, ke

tră ______
flĕ ______
slĭ ______
lŏ ______
dŭ ______

ban ______
mēē ______
sil ______
por ______
dus ______

lā ______
tā ______
spī ______
jō ______
dū ______

(ch)

//tch, ch

bă ______
strĕ ______
dĭ ______
nŏ ______
hŭ ______

mar ______
bēē ______
pin ______
cou ______
mul ______

(j)

//dge, ge

că ______
lĕ ______
brĭ ______
dŏ ______
jŭ ______

pā ______
ver ______
frin ______
stōō ______
gou ______

Code and read these words.

ue = ($\bar{u}$)

One syllable	Two syllables
blue	accrue
clue	ague
cue	argue
due	endue
flue	ensue
glue	imbue
hue	indue
rue	pursue
sue	rescue
	statue
	subdue
	value
	virtue

Three syllables

avenue

barbecue

continue

residue

retinue

revenue

1. The Danube River is not actually blue.

2. "Did you find any clues, Watson?"

3. That bill is past due.

4. The game began as soon as he sauntered into the pool hall, took the ball from the pocket, and picked up his cue.

5. Try Elmer's. It's a super glue.

6. Bert will rue the day he offered to clean the flue.

7. Will she sue the man who crashed into her car?

8. Grace will subdue her feelings of anger and do what she can to help.

9. Leave your cash in the savings account and interest will accrue.

10. If the speech is good, applause will ensue.

11. The Statue of Liberty holds her torch high and stands tall in the New York harbor.

12. The red and yellow hue of the sunset reflected on the sails.

13. The parade will continue down the treelined avenue, and barbecue will be served in the park.

14. Cicero told us that virtue is its own reward.

15. The hunters will pursue the fox over hill and dale.

16. Will the fireman be able to rescue the child from the burning house?

17. Don't argue about the value of the ring.

18. When the agent came to collect the increased revenue, the tenant objected.

19. Followed by her entire retinuc, the singer swept past the director and out of the hall.

Vocabulary Review — optional

From the words at the top of this page select the ones that are associated with the words at the bottom of the page and copy in the blank.

accrue	due	pursue
barbecue	flue	rescue
blue	glue	revenue
clue	hue	statue

1. sky ____________________
2. high ____________________
3. ____________________of Liberty
4. interest will ____________________
5. sooty ____________________
6. ____________________career
7. bright ____________________
8. sea ____________________
9. bill is ____________________
10. ____________________ beef or pork
11. find ____________________
12. sticks like ____________________

Copy these words into the correct column on the following pages.

fade	quake
acorn	humid
sheet	flee
siren	pray
crow	use
clover	paper
hue	deep
game	puny
tumult	quite
duke	pale
quinine	impede
three	value
demon	note
gray	lady
rodent	fee
continue	ether
portray	relay
spume	pole
like	maple
arrow	below

Copy these words into the correct column on the following pages.

may	complete
viper	mane
rebate	canine
ampere	creed
seed	spree
side	tirade
bellow	file
grow	profile
shy	convene
female	cue
locust	code
slogan	lope
cry	spry
rope	mute
cupid	sty
argue	trident
pupil	tee
muse	sequin
my	effete
grime	heel

(ā)

a – e	a	ay

(ē)

ee	e – e	e	ee

(ī)

i – e	i	y

(ō)

o — e	o	ow

(ū)

u — e	u	ue

Read these nonsense words which are similar to the real words for reading found in Bench Mark Measures IIIB.

gleckle	imborm
proe	oncreach
goap	becoyer
worchy	birge
raunt	spow
quoasy	gredge
dalk	millow
daucem	amfue
venquith	gleaden
tacaw	hunage